The Marlin and the Mermaid ™
Investigate
"The Great Pacific Garbage Patch"

Based on characters created by Daniel R. Ford

Written by Daniel R. Ford

Paula Tortolini - Editor

Lisa McLeod - Cover and interior illustrations

Pete Crossley - Graphics

Published by Green Seahorse Media LLC

Kamalani Anuhea Kalama was born on August 9, 1999 in Kailua, Oahu, Hawaii. She was a student at Kainalu Elementary School and went on to Kailua Intermediate School where she was a leader to all who knew her. She was a mentor, a peer educator, an advocate, and a friend to all. She encouraged positive relationships with all she knew. Kamalani was also an athlete who enjoyed hiking, soccer, volleyball, and most especially ocean sports. Through her participation on the Kailua Canoe Club, Kamalani brought her strong connection to the ocean and her inspirational skills together. She encouraged her teammates during practices and races to never give up. Kamalani's love for the ocean was more than just a paddle in the water; she strived for teamwork, safety, and conservation of the aina (land) and the kai (water). The Kalama family has a strong history in the paddling community and Kamalani perpetuated this.

Malama pono a hui hou. "Take care, until we meet again sweet angel."

Look inside for Mermaid Kamalani

"Where ever Life takes Me,
You will always find Me
with a Smile"........Kamalani

Kamalani Anuhea Kalama
August 9th, 1999-May 5th, 2013

I would like to give special thanks to Lisa, Paula, and Pete who helped create, revise, and format this book. Their dedication and passion in their areas of expertise helped pull this project together. I will always be grateful!

Editor, Paula Tortolini
Paula Tortolini spent her career as an elementary school educator, curriculum designer, and staff developer. In retirement, she serves as a literacy consultant, and she continues her work with children as a teacher on the Reading Bus, a Virginia Beach City Public Schools early intervention program.

Artist, Lisa McLeod
Drawing and creating art since picking up a pencil as a child, I received formal training from The Art Institute for a couple of summers. I've dabbled in fantasy and realism over the years; outside of painting and drawing I enjoy reading. My favorite writers are Neil Gaimon, John Green, Jack London, Stephen King, Allen Moore, and recently H.P Lovecraft. I also love graphic novels and choice comic books. When I have time I can really tear up a good video game.

Graphic Designer, Peter Crossley
A graphic artist with over 25 years' experience in print and design, educated in the UK at Kitson College of Printing. Pete was introduced to bird and wildlife watching by his grandfather as a child. He would like for his kids to have the same passion for wildlife preservation and conservation and feels this series of stories is a great way to bring that message, not only to his but all kids and adults alike.

Author, Daniel R. Ford
The character's voyage to the Great Pacific Garbage Patch is based on a similar route I sailed to the Pacific Ocean and the Hawaiian coast back in the mid 1990's. Those experiences have helped guide my mission to help educate children on the importance for sustaining a healthy Ocean.

THE MERMAID's CLOSET

The mission for Green Seahorse Media LLC is to help educate readers on the Marine environment, to foster a love for our waters, and promote sustainability for this natural resource.

Further information may be obtained by reaching the Author or Publisher, Green Seahorse Media LLC at info@gsh-media.com

Green Seahorse Media LLC publications are available for special promotional and premium uses and may be created for customized editions. For further in-formation please contact promotions@gsh-media.com

Library of Congress Cataloging-in-Publication Data
Ford, Daniel R., 1961-
The Marlin and the Mermaid
Investigate "The Great Pacific Garbage Patch"
Daniel R. Ford
LCCN: 2013950801
ISBN: 978-0-9855295-3-6
Copyright Registration Number: Txu 1-861-941 April 5th, 2013

The Marlin and the Mermaid Investigate

"The Great Pacific Garbage Patch"

**This story starts along Virginia's coast
in our nation's largest estuary.**

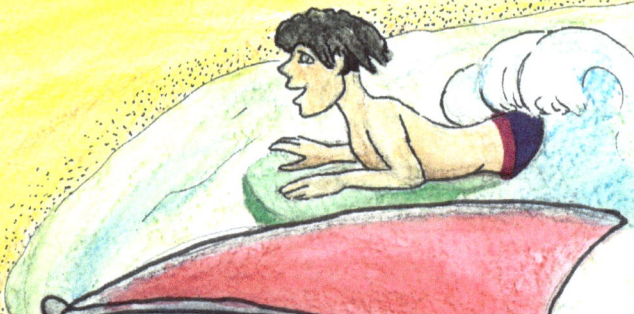

The Marlin and the Mermaid
Were reading, relaxing, and enjoying the day
Hanging loose in their favorite nook
The Chesapeake Bay.

FILTER FRIENDS

MEAN CLEAN MACHINE

The water was cleaner.
The bay was becoming
free of debris.

THE INTERESTING NEWS.

All of the people were working together.
It was a wonderful sight to see.

Then they read a troubling article
About fishes, birds, turtles, dolphins, and whales
Being harmed by plastic pollution
That they ate or got tangled in their tails.

Far out in the Pacific Ocean
In an area called a gyre
Lay a vast expanse of plastic trash.
The problem seemed quite dire!

Great Pacific
Garbage Patch

Hawaiian
Islands

N

FALSE CAPE

CAPE HATTERAS

CAPE CANAVERAL

OIL RIG

Key West

CARIBBEAN SEA

So they decided to venture
Out to the West Coast
To conduct an investigation
And locate this harmful host.

PANAMA CANAL

They grabbed a compass
And charted the course.
The Mermaid whistled for "Butter Run"
Her Giant Seahorse.

The group started south
Along Virginia's False Cape
Past pristine beaches
And beautiful seascape.

Cape Hatteras was next
As they continued on their trip.
Considered the graveyard of the Atlantic
This location has claimed many a ship.

This is where the Labrador Current
And Gulf Stream collide.
Two strong bodies of water converge
To create a turbulent downside.

LABRADOR CURRENT

GULF STREAM

Southwest to Cape Canaveral
Rich in space history, they say.
Behind lies Mosquito Lagoon
Where ancient manatees play.

Merritt
Island

Swimming into the Gulf of Mexico
They maintained their steady pace
Past an infamous location
Where our Nation's worst oil spill took place.

Voyaging to the Caribbean Sea
Where whale sharks swim in style
The trio was astonished
By the enormity of each shark's smile!

They arrived at the Panama Canal
An amazing historic feat!
Theodore Roosevelt, a U.S. President,
Helped make this passageway complete.

They transited through the canal
With three locks up and three locks down
Until they reached the West Coast
To the "Garbage Patch" they were bound.

Between Hawaii and California
Is the area called a gyre.
This is "The Great Pacific Garbage Patch"
Where trash floats in a mire.

Ghost nets and plastic trash,
Oily sludge and marine debris,
Litter this large region
As far as the eye can see.

Plastic bags look like jellyfish
To sea turtles swimming by.

Bottle caps resemble little fish
To an Albatross in the sky.

Fishermen's nets offer a special allure
To playful dolphins jumping near.
These dangerous, dangling traps
Are hazards these mammals should fear!

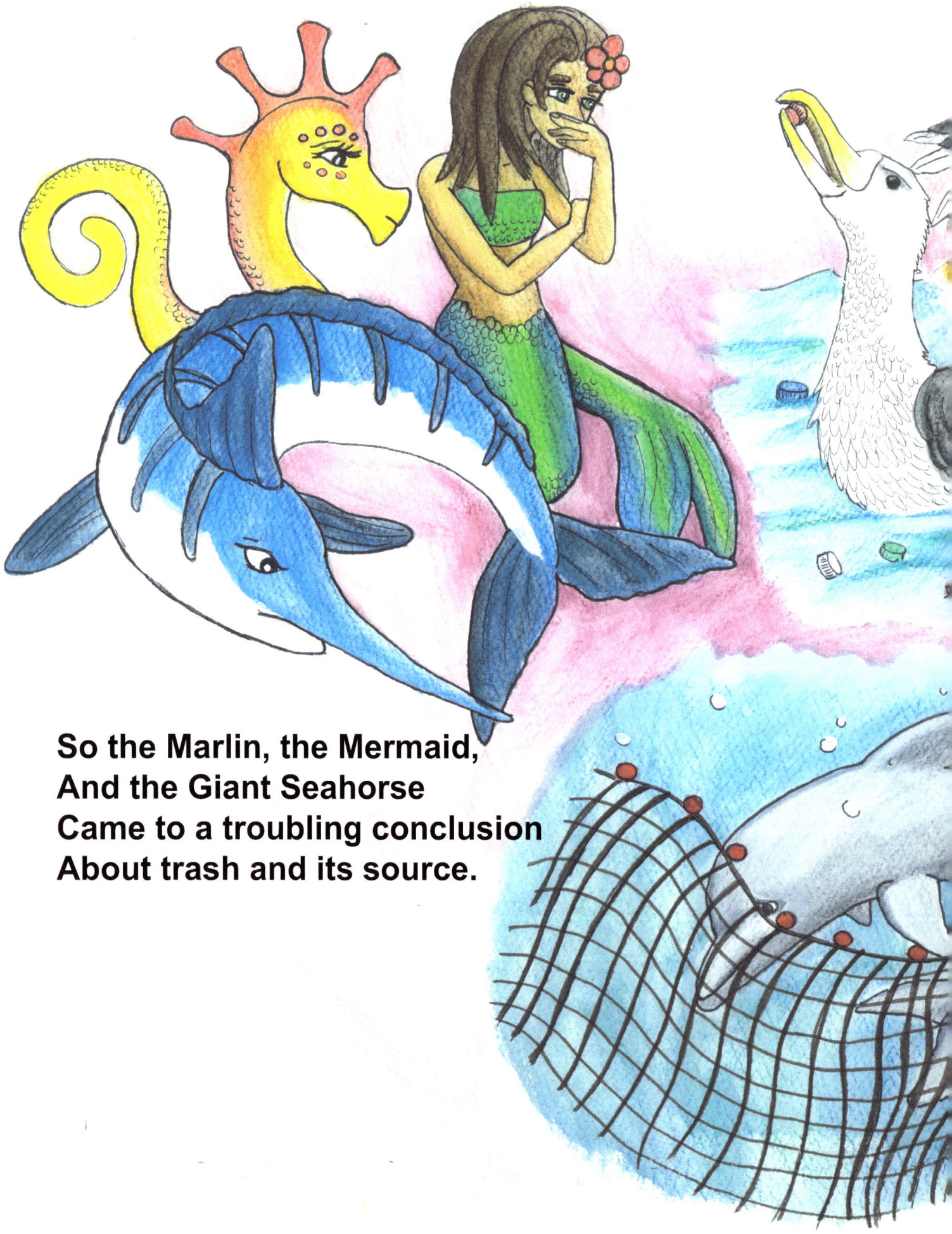

So the Marlin, the Mermaid,
And the Giant Seahorse
Came to a troubling conclusion
About trash and its source.

From their investigation
They discovered this fact:
*The pollution in our oceans
Has a negative impact.*

That float in our rivers,
And into our Bays,
Out to our oceans,
And Far, Far Away?

Interesting Science Facts

Albatross: A large web-footed sea bird with long, narrow wings and a hooked beak. The albatross has a wing span of twelve feet, drinks salt water, and can survive out at sea for five to ten years.

Blue Whale: A marine mammal that is bluish-grey in color. The largest animal on earth, the blue whale can grow to 100 feet in length, weigh up to 200 tons, and shoot water from its spout thirty feet in the air.

Clown Fish: Also called anemone fish, the clown fish is bright orange with white stripes. This fish is found in tropical waters throughout the world.

Dolphin: A marine mammal, closely related to the whale and porpoise. The carnivorous dolphin is a highly intelligent animal that uses echo location for hunting food and communicates by whistling and clicking. The largest dolphin is a killer whale.

Horseshoe Crab: A hard-shelled, invertebrate that lives on the sea floor of shallow coastal waters. The horseshoe crab is not really a crab; it is more closely related to arachnids, such as scorpions and spiders. Female horseshoe crabs lay between 60,000 and 120,000 eggs, and the blood of the horseshoe crab is blue.

Manatee: A sluggish, aquatic mammal found in the coastal waters of Florida, the Gulf of Mexico, and the West Indies. Also referred to as a sea cow, the manatee can grow up to thirteen feet in length and can weigh up to 1200 pounds. The manatee is an endangered species.

Manta Ray: The largest species of ray, the manta ray spans over twenty feet across and weighs over 2500 pounds. The manta ray lives in warm water and is made entirely of cartilage.

Pelican: A sea bird that has a long beak and large throat pouch used to store fish. The wing span of the pelican can reach ten feet.

Sea Turtle: A sea turtle lays its eggs on the beach in clutches of 50 to 200. Sea turtles can be found around the world, and most are on the endangered species list. The leatherback, the largest of the seven species, can weigh over 1,000 pounds.

Whale Shark: The world's largest fish, this filter-feeder is as long as a school bus (over forty foot), weighs over twenty tons, can live to be seventy, and is found in warm waters around the world.

Wonderful Resources

www.virginiaaquarium.com

VIRGINIA
AQUARIUM
& MARINE SCIENCE CENTER

www.montereybayaquarium.org

Monterey Bay Aquarium®

www.waikikiaquarium.org

WAIKIKI
AQUARIUM
UNIVERSITY OF HAWAI'I

www.aquariumofpacific.org

"Authors Notes"

It is our responsibility to protect the Marine Environment and all its inhabitants which were created for us!

Kamalani Anuhea Kalama

In the beginning of the summer, while searching for a Hawaiian woman to use as a model for the next mermaid, I noticed Kamalani's picture on a friend's Facebook page. (I was trying to find a picture for Lisa, our illustrator, to use as a basis for the creation of this mermaid.)

After hearing of the story of Kamalani, my heart was moved. I wanted to create a mermaid in Kamalani's likeness, but felt compelled to create "Mermaid Kamalani" as a separate mermaid, with her own message and story.

Mermaid Kamalani is introduced in the book with a pair of green sea turtles. In Hawaii, sea turtles represent "Protectors and Guardians" and, as such, hold special significance in Hawaiian culture.

With this in mind, and God willing, my goal is to develop a story where Mermaid Kamalani and the Giant Green Sea Turtles will help educate the public and cultivate future leaders to help protect our marine environment and its natural resources.

This book honors the life of Kamalani Anuhea Kalama, a young Woman whose joyful spirit was embraced by all who knew her!

www.ingramcontent.com/pod-product-compliance
Lightning Source LLC
Chambersburg PA
CBHW060832270326

41933CB00002B/64